Jame Allison Searight

In Loving Memory of a Revered Father and a Sainted Mother

Jame Allison Searight

In Loving Memory of a Revered Father and a Sainted Mother

ISBN/EAN: 9783337114473

Printed in Europe, USA, Canada, Australia, Japan

Cover: Foto ©Lupo / pixelio.de

More available books at **www.hansebooks.com**

Wm Searight

IN LOVING MEMORY

OF

A REVERED FATHER

AND

A SAINTED MOTHER.

WILLIAM SEARIGHT.

THE wonderful Scotch-Irish race, in its career
among the nations of the earth, has been fitly
compared to the Gulf Stream in its course through
the regions of the ocean. To trace the making of
the Scotch-Irishman we must go back to the centuries before the Christian era, during one of which
a branch of the Gallic or Celtic race from the wild
interior of Asia, settled in Asia Minor, which it
named Gallatia. This restless Gallic people soon
left Asia, and passed through Italy, Spain and
Southern France, to which it gave the name of
Gaul, and settled in Great Britain, where it became
the Celtic race of the British Isles. The branches
that settled in Ireland and Scotland soon came to
be known as Scots. In 430 the famous St. Patrick,
a Scotsman of patrician birth, made Ireland the
field of his wonderful religious labors, and one
hundred and twenty years later St. Columba, an
Irishman of Scot blood, and of the royal lineage of
the house of Ulster, founded in the Scottish island
of Iona, on the ruins of an old Druid college, the
college of Icolmkill, which shed its rays of light

3

all over Europe during the darkness of the Middle Ages. Three centuries after the founding of this great college came the occupation of the seed bed of the Scotch-Irish race, which lies in the water-girt region embracing the southern part of the lowlands of Scotland, then known as Stathclyde: and the river-encircled plain of northern England, which at that time bore the name of Northumbria. Into this peculiar region came the Dalriadaian Scot from the north of Ireland in large numbers to absorb its few Celtic inhabitants who were descendants of the ancient Britons of King Arthur's days. The boldest of the Vikings and Sea Kings sailed up the rivers of this land and left many of their bravest followers to become a part of a new forming race by infusing into it the best blood of the Norseman, the Dane and the Saxon. This Brito-Scot and Anglo-Norman fusion formed a people known as the Lowland Scot, who, from 1047 to 1605, were passing through a fixing period in which they assumed a new character under the preaching of John Knox, and made their name famous all through Europe as the fighting grandsons of the "old raiders of the North." In 1605 the Lowland Scot was ready for transplanting by the Divine Husbandman, and on April 16, 1605, the English court signed the charter to colonize Ulster or the North of Ireland with the Bible-reading Lowland Scot and the choicest blood of England. The Lowland Scot stock in Ulster was modified by the choicest elements of the Puritan, the Huguenot and Hollander, and thus became the Ulsterman, noted for thrift, prudence and prosperity. He made a war-worn desert a fertile land, and then finding himself persecuted by the government, he changed from the contented colonist to the exasperated Scotch-Irish emigrant. By persecution the Ulsterman was made ready for his mission in the new world, where, settling on the western frontier of the Thirteen Colonies, he became the Scotch-Irishman of history, so named from the dominating strain of his blood and the land from which he had come. He protected the settlement from the Indians; he bore an important part in the revolutionary struggle for Independence, and he was mainly instrumental in winning all of the territory of the United States north of the Ohio and west of the Mississippi river. The Scotch-Irish is a grand race, whose great characteristics are: Independence, education, and Scriptural faith. The Scotch-Irish have always borne a prominent and distinguished part in the progress of the Union, from its establishment down to the present time, and being the "first to start and the last to quit," can proudly say "my past is my pledge to the future."

5

Of this great race came William Searight, the subject of the first of these two memoirs.

William Searight, of Menallen township, the founder of the Fayette county family of Searights, was born near Carlisle, Cumberland county, Pennsylvania, December 5, 1791. He was of Scotch-Irish descent on both paternal and maternal sides. His family came from Scotland, and had for its crest a hand holding a thunderbolt, while its motto was *Deum Time*. His paternal grandfather, William Seawright, came from near Londonderry, in County Donegal, in the North of Ireland, about the year 1740, settled in Lampiter township, Lancaster county, Pennsylvania, and was, at the time of his death, 1771, a prominent citizen and landholder of that county. His paternal grandmother, Anne Hamilton, came from Belfast, Ireland, at the same time, and settled in about the same locality near Lancaster city, Pennsylvania. She came to America with her brothers William and Hugh, and a sister Mary. Her brother William was the grandfather of the distinguished governor of South Carolina in Calhoun's day, who was known as the Nullifier Governor, in consequence of his having advocated the nullification of certain tariff laws passed by Congress, which he considered adverse to the interests of the people of the South. A pretty full though incomplete history of the Hamilton family of Lancaster county, this State, can be seen in Egles' Pennsylvania Genealogies and in "Notes and Queries," by Colonel Evans, of Columbia. The ancestors of the Lancaster county Hamilton family, of which, as stated, the grandmother of the subject of this memorial was a member, went from Scotland to Belfast, Ireland, when it became the refuge for persecuted Covenanters. They were a part of the historical Scotch family of Hamiltons, one of whom was chosen as the husband of Queen Mary, and another as the husband of Queen Elizabeth. Family tradition and family history also teach that Alexander Hamilton of revolutionary fame was connected with this same Lancaster county family of Hamiltons.

The names of the children of William Seawright and Anne Hamilton were Mary, Esther, Anne, William (the father of the subject of this first memorial), and Alexander. (See deed book W. W., page 134, Lancaster county records.)

Mary, the eldest of the children, married John Glenn. The Glenns are extinct, and mostly sleep in Cumberland county, Pennsylvania.

Esther married Gilbert Seawright, and did not change her name. Gilbert Seawright was the founder of the large family of Seawrights in and around Carlisle, Cumberland county, this State.

7

Anne married William Woods and removed from Lancaster county to Albemarle county, Virginia, where they died. They had two children: Alexander and Seawright, who were born in Lancaster county, this State. These children settled in Fayette county, Kentucky, and afterward removed to Illinois, where Alexander died in Jo Daviess county, and Seawright passed away in Greene county.

Alexander married a Logan, and removed to Augusta county, Virginia. They had three children: William, Alexander, and Margaret, who removed with their families from Augusta county, Virginia, to Henry county, Tennessee, in about the year 1826, where some of their descendants are now living.

William married Jean Ramsey, a daughter of Samuel and Catherine Ramsey (*nee* Seawright).

The maternal great-grandfather of William Searight came from Donegal, Ireland, about 1740, and settled in Leacock township, near Lancaster city, Pennsylvania, where he lived and died. His name was also William Seawright. He was for many years a landholder and prominent citizen of Lancaster county, this State. In the Revolution of 1688, the ancestors of William Seawright threw themselves into the cause of William of Orange. Some of them were driven within the walls of Londonderry when its gates were closed against James the Second, some afterwards died in the besieged city, while others of them survived the siege. The maternal great-grandmother of the subject of this first memorial was also a resident of the North of Ireland. Her maiden name was Catherine Jackson. William Seawright and Catherine Jackson had but one child, Catherine. Catherine Seawright married Samuel Ramsey, of Lancaster county, Pennsylvania, who afterwards became a wealthy and prominent citizen of Cumberland county, this State. He owned the famous "Letort Springs" tract near Carlisle, where he lived and died. They were the parents of the mother of the subject of this first memorial. The names of the children of Samuel and Catherine (Seawright) Ramsey were: Jean, Catherine, Margaret, Esther, Elizabeth, Samuel, Archibald and Seawright. Jean married William Seawright. Catherine, Margaret, Esther and Elizabeth died unmarried. Samuel married a Gettysburg lady and had no children. Archibald married Margaret Dean, some of whose grandchildren are now residents of New Bloomfield, Perry county, Pennsylvania. Seawright Ramsey married a Denny, a member of the Pittsburgh family of Dennys, and a sister of the wife of the late Dr. Murray, of Carlisle, this State. All of this family except Jean and Samuel sleep in the old graveyard at Carlisle, Pennsylvania.

Samuel is interred in Huntingdon county, this State, and Jean in the Ligonier valley. After the death of his wife Catherine, Samuel Ramsey married the widow Macfeely, grandmother of General Robert Macfeeley, commissary general, United States Army, of Washington, District of Columbia.

In about 1780 the parents of William Searight removed from Lancaster to Cumberland county, Pennsylvania, and from there to Augusta county, Virginia. They remained in Virginia about eight years, when they returned to Cumberland county. There they remained for a short time, when they started for the western part of the State, stopping a short time in Huntingdon and Indiana counties, and finally made their permanent settlement in the Ligonier valley, Westmoreland county, Pennsylvania, about five miles above Ligonier, on the Loyalhanna river.

The names of the brothers and sisters of William Searight were: Samuel, Alexander, Mary, John, Hamilton and Archibald. After 1810 Samuel settled in Tippecanoe county, Indiana. Alexander first settled in Brooke county, Virginia, and afterwards removed to Morgan county, Ohio, and William, the subject of this first memorial, settled in Fayette county, Pennsylvania. The other members of the family remained in the Ligonier valley, and died without issue, and their remains lie beside their parents in "Pleasant Grove" graveyard, about five miles from the town of Ligonier.

William Searight received only a plain English education, but he was endowed with the precepts of stern integrity, industry, sobriety, and honor, the elements of his future success in business, and of his elevated character. In the neighborhood in which he was reared, he had learned the business of fuller and dyer of cloth, a knowledge of which, with his energy, sobriety and honor, was his entire stock in hand. He arrived in Fayette county at about the age of twenty-one, and commenced business at an old fulling-mill on Dunlap's creek, known as Hammond's mill. He afterwards prosecuted his vocation at Cooke's mill, on Redstone creek at the mouth of Dunlap's creek, and also on the old George Washington farm, near Perryopolis. He next purchased a farm and hotel at Searights, the property and village deriving its name from him, and there made his permanent settlement. On March 26, 1826, he married Rachel Brownfield, a daughter of Thomas and Elizabeth Brownfield, of Uniontown, Pennsylvania.

Rachel Brownfield (wife of William Searight) was of English Quaker lineage. Her parents were natives of Frederick county, Virginia. Her memorial, which follows, will contain an account of her ancestry.

11

At the village of Searights, William Searight laid the foundation of a large fortune. His integrity, united to a generous and benevolent heart, gave him a high place in the esteem and affections of the community in which he lived. His sound judgment soon impressed itself on his own county and he became one of her most influential and useful citizens. He was a prominent and zealous old-time Democratic politician, and wielded a wide influence. On one occasion he rode on horseback from Searights to Harrisburgh, a distance of over two hundred miles, to assist in the preparation to nominate General Jackson for the presidency. He was an intimate friend of the late Simon Cameron, ex-United States senator from Pennsylvania, and had close political relations with the leading politicians of his day.

In the early history of Fayette county, political conventions of both parties were accustomed to meet at Searights and plan campaigns. A memorable meeting, of which Mr. Searight was the chief promoter, was held there in 1828, known as the " Gray Meeting," from the name of the keeper at that time of the local hotel, John Gray. At this meeting the Jackson and Adams men met to test their strength. They turned out in the meadow below the hotel, formed in rank and counted off; the Jackson men outnumbered their opponents decisively, and it was regarded as a great Jackson victory.

In the political campaign of 1856 a large democratic meeting was held at Uniontown, and the delegation from Searights bore a banner with the inscription "Menallen the battle ground of the Gray Meeting." Many politicians of the olden time were at the Gray Meeting, among them on the Jackson side were General Henry W. Beeson, Colonel Ben Brownfield, Westley Frost, William F. Coplan, Henry J. Rigden, James C. Beckley, Benedict Kimber, Solomon G. Krepps, William Searight, Hugh Keys, William Hatfield, Colonel William L. Miller, John Fuller, Provance McCormick, William Davidson, Alexander Johnson and Thomas Duncan. On the Adams side were Andrew Stewart, John M. Austin, F. H. Oliphant, John Kennedy, John Dawson, William P. Wells, Samuel Evans, James Bowman, Stokely Connell, William Hogg, Basil Brownfield, George Mason, Kennedy Duncan and John Lyon.

The many similar political meetings with which William Searight was identified, go to show the esteem in which he was held by the citizens of the county by all parties. But Fayette county, although the first, was but little in advance of other counties to learn and admire his worth. He early became known and appreciated throughout the entire State.

14

He was appointed commissioner of the Cumberland road (National road) by Governor Porter in the most palmy days of that great thoroughfare, a position he held for many years. In 1845 he was superseded by Colonel William Hopkins, of Washington, Pennsylvania. Subsequently an act of the legislature placed the road in the hands of trustees, appointed by the courts, and these trustees restored William Searight to the commissionership, the duties of which office he continued to discharge with great fidelity and industry. He was thoroughly familiar with all the hills and valleys of that grand old road, once so stirring and active, but now still and grass-grown. Previous to his appointment as commissioner of the National road he was a contractor on the same. He was one of the contractors who built the iron bridge over the mouth of Dunlap's creek, between Bridgeport and Brownsville, and was also a contractor on the Erie extension of the Pennsylvania and Ohio canal.

At the time of his death he was the candidate of the Democratic party for one of the most important offices in the State, that of canal commissioner. To this office he would have undoubtedly been elected, had not death interposed and called him from the active duties of this life to the realities of another world, as after his death Colonel

William Hopkins, of Washington county, was nominated by the Democratic party for the same office, and was elected by a large majority. He died at his residence in Menallen township, on the 12th day of August, 1852. He left a widow and six children: Thomas B., Ewing B., Jean, Captain William, James A., and Elizabeth. His widow, whose memorial follows his own in this volume, died at Uniontown, on January 3, 1893, at the advanced age of eighty-eight years. Of the children, Captain William is dead, the rest are living. Thomas B., Jean and James A. live in Uniontown. Ewing B. lives on the old homestead in Menallen township, and Elizabeth is the wife of J. T. Colvin, President of the Pittsburgh National Bank of Commerce, and lives in Pittsburgh.

William Searight was a man of the most generous and humane character, ever ready to lend his counsel, his sympathies, and his purse to the aid of others. Though a strong political party man, yet he always treated his opponents with courtesy. In religion he was like most of the race to which he belonged, imbued with Calvinism. The brightest traits of his character were exemplified in his last hours. So far as human judgment can decide, he died a Christian. His aged widow often quoted an expression he made as he was approaching the sad realities of death, which gave her much comfort

16

then, and continued to comfort her as her trembling footsteps drew near the shores of the same river, over which he passed so many years ago; it was this: "Our prayers have been answered; I feel that if I should die to-night, the Lord will receive me into His Holy Kingdom." Although death plucked him from the very threshold of earthly honors, yet it caused him no regrets. The Kingdom into which he was about to enter presented higher honors, and purer enjoyments. To him they offered:

"No midnight shade, no clouded sun,
But sacred, high, eternal noon."

A more emphatic eulogy than is in the power of language to express was bestowed upon him on the day of his funeral, by the assembling around his coffin, to perform the last sad duty of friendship, of as great if not a greater number of citizens than ever attended the funeral ceremonies of any one who had died within the limits of Fayette county. Among that vast assemblage were alike the patriarchs of the county and the rising youth who came to give their testimony to the lofty worth in life of the distinguished dead. A few days after his death a large meeting of the citizens of Fayette county, irrespective of party, convened at the court house for the purpose of bearing suitable testimony

17

to his memory and character. The following gentlemen were chosen officers: Hon. Nathaniel Ewing, president: Hon. Daniel Sturgeon (ex-United States senator) and Z. Ludington, vice-presidents; John B. Krepps and R. P. Flenniken, secretaries. On motion of Hon. James Veech (later author of "Monongahela of Old"), a committe on resolutions, composed of leading citizens, was appointed, which committee presented the following preamble and resolutions, which were unanimously adopted:

"When a valuable citizen dies, it is meet that the community of which he was a member mourn his loss. A public expression of their sorrow at such an event is due as some solace to the grief of the bereaved family and friends, and as an incentive to others to earn for their death the same distinction.

"In the recent death of William Searight, this community has lost such a citizen. Such an event has called this public meeting, into which enter no schemes of political promotion, no partisan purposes of empty eulogy. Against all this death has shut the door. While yet the tear hangs upon the cheek of his stricken family, and tidings of his death are unread by many of his friends, we, his fellow citizens, neighbors, friends, of all parties, have assembled to speak to those who knew and

18

loved him best, and to those who knew him not, the words of sorrow and truth, in sincerity and soberness. Therefore as the sense of this meeting,

"*Resolved*, That in the death of William Searight, Fayette county and the commonwealth of Pennsylvania have lost one of their best and most useful citizens. The people at large may not realize their loss, but the community in which he lived, over whose comforts and interests were diffused the influences of his liberality and enterprise, feel it, while his friends, of all classes, parties and professions, to whom he clung, and who clung to him, mourn it.

"*Resolved*, That while we would withhold our steps from the sanctuary of domestic grief, we may be allowed to express to the afflicted widow and children of the deceased our unfeigned sorrow and sympathy in their great bereavement, and to tender them our assurance that while in their hearts the memory of the husband and father will ever be cherished, in our hearts will be kept the liveliest recollections of his virtues as a citizen and a friend.

"*Resolved*, That among the elements which must enter into every truthful estimate of the character of William Searight, are a warm amenity of manner, combined with great dignity of deportment,

19

which were not the less attractive by their plainness and want of ostentation; elevated feelings more pure than passionless; high purposes with untiring energy in their accomplishment; an ennobling sense of honor and individual independence, which kept him always true to himself and to his engagements; unfaltering fidelity to his friends; a liberality which heeded no restraint, but means and merit; great promptness and fearlessness in the discharge of what he believed to be a duty, private or public, guided by a rigid integrity, which stood all tests and withstood all temptations; honesty and truthfulness in word and deed, which no seductions could weaken nor assaults overthrow, in all respects the architect of his own fortune and fame. These, with the minor virtues in full proportion, are some of the outlines of character which stamped the man whose death we mourn, as one much above the ordinary level of his race.

"*Resolved*, That while we have here nothing to do or say as to the loss sustained by the political party to which he belonged, and whose candidate he was for an office of great honor and responsibility, we may be allowed to say that had he lived and been successful, with a heart so rigidly set as was his, with feelings so high and integrity so firm, and withal an amount of practical intelligence so ample as he possessed, his election could have been regretted by no citizen who knew him and who placed the public interests beyond selfish ends and party success. As a politician we knew him to hold to his principles and party predilections with a tenacious grasp, yet he was ever courteous and liberal in his deportment and views towards his political opponents.

"*Resolved*, That in the life and character of William Searight we see a most instructive and encouraging example. Starting in the struggle of life with an humble business poor and unbefriended, with an honest mind and a true heart, with high purposes and untiring industry, he by degrees gained friends and means which never forsook him. He thus won for himself and family ample wealth, and attained a position among his fellow-men which those who have had the best advantages our country affords might well envy. That wealth and that position he used with a just liberality and influence for the benefit of all around and dependent upon him. Though dead, he yet speaketh to every man in humble business — 'Go thou and do likewise, and such shall be thy reward in life and in death.'

"*Resolved*, That the proceedings of this meeting be furnished for publication in all the papers of the county, and a copy thereof, signed by the officers, be presented to the family of the deceased."

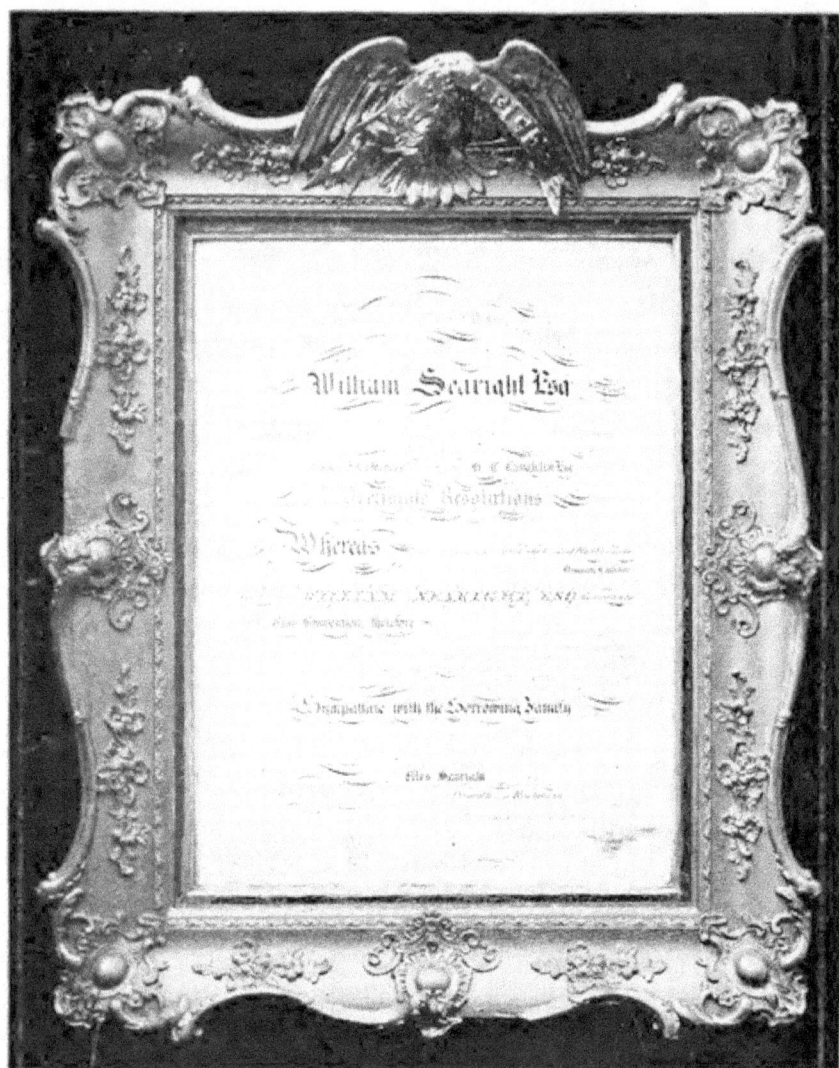

FAC SIMILE OF RESOLUTIONS

Passed by leading democrats of Philadelphia upon learning of the death of William Searight.

The leading democrats of Philadelphia, upon learning of William Searight's death, met and passed resolutions of respect to his many virtues. A copy of these resolutions were beautifully engraved and sent to his family.

A few weeks previous to Mr. Searight's death, the Congressional conferrees of Fayette, Washington and Greene counties met at Waynesburg, and passed resolutions endorsing Pierce and King, Governor Bigler, John L. Dawson, and William Searight. Of Mr. Searight they said:

"*Resolved,* That it shall be our pride and duty to contribute by every honorable means in our power to swell the Democratic majority for our neighbor and well-tried Democrat, WILLIAM SEARIGHT,— candidate for canal commissioner—knowing him to be the very man for the position, and that if elected he will carry into office the same energy, talent, honesty, and kindness of heart which have distinguished him at home in the discharge of his private pursuits."

Among Mr. Searight's papers are found many social invitations from President Buchanan and other men of national fame.

After his death resolutions of condolence were passed at meetings held in adjoining counties, and the press throughout Pennsylvania paid handsome tributes of respect to his life and character.

23

The funeral services of William Searight were conducted by the Rev. Samuel Wilson, founder of Dunlap's Creek Presbyterian academy, and his remains were interred at Grace church, near the village of Searights, under the auspices of the Masonic fraternity, of which he was a member.

William Searight has passed from time to eternity, and left an untarnished name and honorable course in life behind him. Let those who would attain to a like worthy name and useful career, realize that such can only be obtained by energy, industry, economy, honesty and sobriety.

Rachel (Broomfield) Seawright-Sielye.

RACHEL (BROWNFIELD) SEARIGHT-STIDGER.

ONE of the later and most powerful of the races of the human family is the English; and the making of the Englishman can be traced from the cradle and nursery of the human race in Central Asia, away into five great climate zones, around whose settlement centers grew race masses. Three were in Asia, one along the Nile, the other on the shores of the Mediterranean, where civilization had its birth and the two great groups of modern nations, the Latin and the Greek, had their rise. Of the fierce Northland German races, that swept from the Mediterranean to the Baltic, one was Teutonic, whose unconquerable tribes settled largely along the northward waterways from the heart of the great German forest. Three of these tribes, the Angles, Jutes and Saxons, stretched westward along the North Sea coast from the mouth of Elbe River to that of the Weser. Their life was fierce and the land was wild, but both were needed, the one to fashion the earliest character elements of the parent stock of the wonderous Englishman, and

27

the other to render a birthland so uninviting as to drive its children forth to their destiny of an island home and a world-wide dominion. The Britons' appeal for aid against the Pictish invader of Scotland was answered by the grating of Anglican, Saxon, and Jutish boats upon the British shore; but the invited defenders, when the Pict was driven back, became the self-appointed conquerors, and the nursery was exchanged for the school grounds of the oncoming Englishman.

The Angles gave their name to the country, the Saxons theirs to the language, while the Jutes were so few in numbers as to stamp their name in no prominent way and were even denied mention in the name of the new race, which at the time of their conquest by the Normans was called Anglo-Saxon. The Anglo-Saxon had driven the Briton from the land, but when in turn they were conquered by the Dane and Norman they remained, and in one hundred and fifty years had so largely absorbed their last conquerors that there were an Anglo-Saxon and Norman-Dane people that became known as English when they aided the Barons, on June 16th, 1215, to compel King John to sign the Magna Charta, which secured many liberties for all the people of England, which country had formerly been called Angleland. From the granting of the Great Charter the Englishman rapidly developed

28

those magnificent and powerful traits of character for which he is noted all over the world. He warred with Wales and Scotland and France from 1282 to 1450, and in the next hundred years had planted great colonies in the new world. In the meantime the strength of the English people was increasing in the growth of the House of Commons, whose power was instrumental in the destruction of the Feudal nobility in the War of the Roses, but was not powerful enough to restrain the Crown until the days of the Stuarts. Then the great struggle was fought out and Absolute monarchy went down in the great Revolution of 1688, when Constitutional government and a Limited monarchy were established. One year later the Bill of Rights was passed, the Commons was in the ascendancy, and the making of the Englishman was completed. His character was fully formed. He was as unbending as oak, possessed of great fortitude, and had a high sense of honor and a strong love of home and country. Intelligence, genius and decision are his in bountiful measure, and, though sometimes wrong, yet the English have swept forward in a career of greatness among the nations of the earth that has never been equaled in the old, and can only be surpassed in the new world by the United States, the mightiest of England's many planted colonies in the different parts of the globe.

From this wonderful English race was descended Mrs. Rachel (Brownfield) Searight-Stidger, the subject of the second of these two memoirs.

Mrs. Rachel Brownfield Stidger (formerly Searight, widow of William Searight), died at her home at the west end of Main street, Uniontown, Pennsylvania, at fifteen minutes after eight o'clock on Tuesday, January 3, 1893.

Her father, Thomas Brownfield, and her mother, Elizabeth (Fisher) Brownfield, were both natives of Frederick county, Virginia. Their remains are buried in the central part of the old Methodist church burial ground at Uniontown, Pennsylvania, near the grave of Col. William B. Roberts, of Mexican war fame. One infant son and others of her relatives also sleep there. Her grandfather, Barak Fisher, and her grandmother, Mary (Butler) Fisher, were both natives of Bucks county, Pennsylvania, and sleep in the old Back Creek meeting house burial ground, at Gainsboro, Frederick county, Virginia, about nine miles from Winchester. Her grandparents were married in "Buckingham Meeting House," Bucks county, Pennsylvania, on the 18th day of the Second month, 1761. This meeting house has the usual partition or division for the purpose of separating at certain meetings the Orthodox and the Hicksites. In this partition there is a bullet hole made by a ball from a revolutionary gun shot over fifteen years after this marriage took place. At a meeting on the 6th day of the Sixth month, 1763, at Hopewell meeting house, Frederick county, Virginia, there was a certificate produced from Buckingham monthly meeting, in Bucks county, this State, for Barak Fisher and Mary (Butler) Fisher, his wife, which was read and accepted. Hence her grandparents must have removed from Bucks county, Pennsylvania, to Frederick county, Virginia, in the year 1763. They settled on Back creek, near the village of Gainsboro, about nine miles northwest of Winchester, Virginia. The ruins of the old house in which they lived when they first removed from Pennsylvania to Virginia can yet be seen. The old farm upon which they originally settled is still in possession of some of their descendants. Her grandmother, Mary (Butler) Fisher, died in the year 1800. Her grave is still clearly and distinctly marked. Her grandfather, Barak Fisher, died in the year 1784. His grave is not so clearly defined.

The records of Hopewell monthly meeting, of which Back creek meeting was a branch, contain the names of her grandparents and all their children, as plain and distinct as if they had been written but yesterday. So also is the record of her lineage clear back to the origin of the Society of Friends, in the early part of 1600. Her great-grandfather, John Fisher, and her great-grand-mother, Elizabeth (Scarborough) Fisher, natives of Yorkshire, England, sleep in the Buckingham burying ground, near Centreville, Bucks county, this State. Their graves are not very distinctly defined, as the Society of Friends in the very early history of this country did not particularly care to mark the graves of their dead. Her great-grandfather, John Fisher, was born in Barmstone, Yorkshire, England, 1672, Twelfth month, 20th day. He was the eldest son of John and Sarah (Hutchinson) Fisher. He emigrated in 1703, and settled in Bucks county, Pennsylvania. On the 3d day of the Third month, 1710, he married Mary Janney, in Falls meeting house. Mary (Hough-Janney) Fisher was the widow of Jacob Janney. Her maiden name was Hough. Jacob Janney was a relative of Samuel Janney, who was the author of "Janney's History of the Society of Friends" in America. John Fisher and Mary (Hough-Janney) Fisher had one child named Mary. Thomas Maxwell Potts, of Cannonsburg, Pennsylvania, is one of the descendants of this child Mary. John Fisher's first wife lived only a short time. On the 6th day of the Eleventh month, 1719, her great-grandfather, John Fisher, married Elizabeth Scarborough. From this marriage there was a large family of children, of whom Barak Fisher, her

32

grandfather, was the eighth child. The records of Buckingham monthly meeting, and of the Middletown monthly meeting, Bucks county, Pennsylvania, have the names of her grandfather, Barak Fisher, and her grandmother, Mary (Butler) Fisher, and their brothers and sisters plainly and distinctly set forth. These same records also have the names of her great-grandfather, John Fisher, and her great-grandmother, Elizabeth (Scarborough) Fisher, as distinctly shown, whilst the records of Hull monthly meeting in Yorkshire, England, have the names of the parents, and date of marriage, and also the names of the brothers and sisters of her great-grandfather, John Fisher, as clearly written. Her great-grandfather, Thomas Butler, was born at Hanley, on the Thames, England. His first settlement in America was in Middletown, Bucks county, Pennsylvania, after which he removed to Chester, in Delaware county, this State. His certificate is dated Tenth month, 5th day, 1728. On the 4th day of the First month, 1730, he re-deposited his certificate in Middletown monthly meeting, Bucks county, from Chester monthly meeting, Delaware county, Pennsylvania. On the 17th day of the Fourth month, 1731, he married Rebecca Gilbert, in the Middletown meeting house. Thomas Butler and Rebecca (Gilbert) Butler had two children, named Joseph and Mary. Mary married

33

Barak Fisher, and they removed, as has already been stated, from Bucks county, Pennsylvania, to Frederick county, Virginia, in the year 1763, where they raised a large family, one of whom (Elizabeth) was the mother of the subject of this memorial. Thus, through scrupulously kept, carefully preserved and unimpeachable records, the lineage of Rachel (Brownfield) Searight-Stidger is traced back to the origin of the Society of Friends in the early part of 1600. From thence, through equally reliable sources, in Parish and other records, her lineage can be traced into the same family of Fishers of which John Fisher, Bishop of Rochester, who was beheaded by Henry VIII. in the early part of the year 1535, was a member. Through her grandmother, Mary Butler, her lineage is also traceable through the same reliable sources, into the family of which Bishop Butler, of Butler's Analogy fame, was a member. The alleged cause of the beheading of John Fisher, Bishop of Rochester, by Henry VIII., was because the Bishop refused to declare his marriage to Anne Boleyn legal. Persistently refusing to affirm its legality, the Bishop was committed to the tower, and treated with great barbarity. Pope Paul III., as a reward for his services, sent the Bishop a Cardinal's hat, and when King Henry was informed of this, he exclaimed: "Mother of God, he shall wear it on his shoulders, then, for

34

I will leave him never a head to set it on." After a brief trial for treason, he was condemned and barbarously beheaded.

Rachel Brownfield Stidger (formerly Searight) was born at the village of Gainesborough, Frederick county, Virginia, on the 7th day of February, 1805. When she was about six weeks old her parents removed from Virginia to Uniontown, Fayette county, Pennsylvania. Her father and mother, her sisters Catherine, Rebecca, Sarah and Mary, and her brother Ewing and herself constituted the family at that time. They came from Gainesborough through Romney over what was known as the old mail route road, and over the same route which General Braddock had come some fifty years before on his disastrous campaign through the mountains toward Fort Duquesne. They traveled the old Braddock road until they came to "Slacks," on top of Laurel Hill, near Washington's Springs. From Slacks (now Washington's Springs) they came to Uniontown over the old Nemacolin road. When they came over the mountains, in 1805, the only stopping places on the old Braddock road, between Uniontown and Cumberland, were, viz.: Slacks, now Washington's Springs; Clements, near Farmington; Clarks, the Burnt Cabins, just back of Squire Smith's; Smiths, at the ferry, now Smithfield; Boughs, one mile east of Smiths; Simpkins, seven miles east of Boughs; Tomlinsons, the Little Meadows; Musselmans, now Frostburg; Gwins, at the forks of the road, the left road going to Cumberland, and the right road to Romney and Winchester. Sarah, the third child, relict of the late Dennis Springer, of North Union township, recently deceased at the age of ninety-four years, frequently said that whilst they were on the way from Virginia to Uniontown they stopped at what was called the "Burnt Cabins," or "Clarks," and spent Easter day. Sarah was about eight years of age at that time, and up to the time of her death, in 1891, she recollected distinctly that her parents sent out and got a basket of Easter eggs, and that they had an Easter egg feast at the "Burnt Cabins" on Easter of the year 1805. The "Burnt Cabins" was on the old Braddock road not far from the line between Henry Clay and Wharton townships, Fayette county, Pennsylvania, where, in 1790, a man named Clark lived, and which on the old road was called "Clarks." In 1796 David Young kept tavern there. The ruins of the old stone chimney and a splendid spring of the coldest water are the only things left to mark its site. As Easter Sunday in 1805 fell upon the 14th day of April, the family was at the "Burnt Cabins" at that date, en route for Uniontown. They arrived in Uniontown on the 18th or 19th day of April, 1805. The house in

36

which the subject of this memorial was born in Virginia is still standing. The old stone chimney is crumbling, but the house is still in a pretty good state of preservation. The old homestead, also, where she landed in Uniontown, an infant of but a few weeks of age, is still standing, and is one of the landmarks of the olden time. It is located at the west end of Main street, and for many years has been owned and occupied by her youngest brother, Nathaniel Brownfield. Her education consisted of all that Uniontown could afford at that time. She went to school in a school room in the old Methodist church which stood on the site of the property now owned by William McShane, on the west end of Peter street. In her girlhood days she sang in the Methodist church choir in this old church. Her mother was a member of the "Society of Friends," but as there was no meeting house of that denomination near enough to attend, she connected herself, after their arrival in Uniontown, with the Methodist church, and continued a consistent and faithful member of that church until her death in 1835. William McCleary, the eldest son of her eldest daughter, Catherine, and who now, at seventy-nine years of age, resides on Church street, at Uniontown, says that when a boy he used to frequently drive with his grandmother out to Sandy Hill "meeting house," in Menallen township, which has long since been abandoned by the Society of Friends. The late William Wilson, the banker, has often stated that Elizabeth Brownfield died one of the most saintly deaths that he had ever witnessed. Her daughter Rachel, the subject of this second memorial, and also her other children, were constant attendants in childhood at the Methodist church. Her brother John, late of South Bend, Indiana, and her sister Hannah and family, of the same place, together with others of her brothers and sisters, have been very faithful and prominent members of the Methodist church. Rachel, however, never united with the M. E. church. In the year 1825, when General Marquis de LaFayette visited Uniontown, Rachel was one of the young girls who were selected to be dressed in white and to precede the escorting procession and strew flowers in the pathway of the distinguished guest.

On March 25, 1826, she was united in marriage to William Searight, of Menallen township, Fayette county, to which place she removed immediately after her marriage. Her first married life home was on the old Nemacolin road, which left the old Braddock road at "Slacks," on top of Laurel Hill, and passed through Uniontown to Brownsville. Her home was situated on this road about an eighth of a mile north of the present village of Searights, in Menallen township. She soon, however, removed from this location on to the then new (now old) National road, and into the village of Searights. Here she lived until the homestead was built, into which she moved and where she resided during the remainder of the days that she spent in Menallen township.

On August 12, 1852, William Searight, her husband, died, yet she still continued to occupy the homestead until the year 1858, at which time she married Harmon Stidger, M. D., of Canton, Ohio, and removed with him to that city. She resided in Canton during the civil war, and watched its progress with great interest. Her son William was a captain in the 8th Pennsylvania reserves, and was reported very sick while the regiment laid upon the river near Fredericksburg, Virginia, and she hastened to his bedside to minister unto him. On this occasion she had a letter direct from the hand of the great war secretary, Edwin M. Stanton. It was also on this trip that she saw Abraham Lincoln on horseback. He was, in company with some of the cabinet, reviewing the troops which were stationed near Fredericksburg, Virginia. After returning from her trip she frequently remarked upon the length of the great war president's back, as she saw him on a splendid charger, towering above his cabinet and guards. When coming up the Potomac she took occasion to speak and minister tenderly to many of the sick and wounded soldiers who were on the boat. When the nation was draped in mourning because of the tragic death of the illustrious president, she reluctantly joined this great populace in submiting to the will of Him whose government is past understanding. Later on, when President Garfield was shamefully assassinated, the tenderness of her heart and the nobleness of her character were again shown forth in her great grief because of that sad affair. So interested was she in this matter that she was always impatient to see and read the bulletins as they told of his painful suffering, until the end came. She was equally interested in reading the trial of his assassin, and joined the nation in landing the justice that led to his final removal. She lived in Canton until the year 1869, at which time she purchased what is known as the "Robert's property," situated at the west end of Main street, Uniontown, Pennsylvania, and returned to Fayette county, this State, and to the old town in which she had passed her earlier days, to live the remainder of her life amongst her old friends and early acquaintances, and from the year 1869 until her death, lived within one hundred feet of the spot on which she landed in 1805, an infant in her mother's arms. Soon after her first marriage and removal to Menallen township to live, she became a member of Grace Episcopal church, in

40

Menallen township, and continued a faithful member of the Episcopal church during her whole after life. She was confirmed by Bishop Onderdonk, whilst the Rev. Mr. Freeman was Rector of Christ church, Brownsville.

Before the building of the present Grace church at Menallen, Episcopal services were frequently held at her home. After the completion of the present church building, we are carried back in youthful memory to a group of male members on one side of the aisle and a group of female members on the other side. Old Robert Jackson, who donated the ground upon which the church stands, and also the graveyard in which the dust of many of these two groups is buried, stood with trembling limbs among those on the right side of the aisle. Old Philip Fout, with his long cue, a part of the dress of those days, with quivering voice and trembling hands, was there also, and started the tunes to "A Charge to keep I have," and "When I can read my title clear," and other old and familiar hymns. James Allison, the old postmaster, whose name is the synonym of honesty and integrity, was there trying to help the singing along in his feeble way, as well as he knew how. Hiram Jackson, John Dixon and the Moores, from near New Salem, were also heartily joining in the service. On the left of the aisle there was a group of females. Amongst this saintly

41

group were Mrs. Hugh Keys, Mrs. John Dixon, Mrs. William Searight (the subject of this second memorial), Mrs. Hiram Jackson, Miss Moore and others. Many of the persons who composed these hallowed groups have long since passed into the heavenly world. Others of them have passed over the river more recently, and now the last member of these groups, Mrs. Searight, has bowed to the incomprehensible summons, and joins the others in the heaven above in possibly singing the same old beautiful and angelic hymns they sang at Grace, Menallen.

The names of the brothers and sisters of Mrs. Searight were as follows: Catherine, who married Ewing McCleary, was the mother of our townsman, William McCleary. Rebecca, married German D. Hair, who came from Lancaster county to Fayette county, this State, during the time the National road was being built. German D. Hair was a schoolmate and always a great friend and admirer of James Buchanan. He was a contractor and builder of many of the beautiful and substantial stone bridges which yet grace the old National road. Sarah, married Dennis Springer, late of North Union township, Fayette county, Pennsylvania. Dennis Springer descended from one of the oldest families in the country. He came of a family which can trace its lineage back to the fifth century. Mary, married

Charles Wolverton, who removed in the early part of this century to Missouri, where he raised a large and widely known family. Ewing, who was well known in Fayette county as one of the oldest and most highly respected merchants, and as President of the People's Bank of Fayette county. Thomas, who was for many years a resident of Henry Clay township, and who at one time was sheriff of Fayette county, and who afterwards removed to Missouri, where he died, highly respected by all who knew him. John, who removed at an early date to South Bend, Indiana, where he became a very prominent citizen and wealthy merchant and banker. Financial troubles, however, overtook him in the latter part of his life, but never swerved him from the path of honesty and integrity. He became a prominent, active and influential member of the Methodist church, and in his palmy days was also somewhat distinguished as a politician. Nathaniel is now, and has been since his birth, a resident of Uniontown, and owns and occupies the old Brownfield homestead at the west end of Main street, and is known by all men to be honest and straightforward in all his dealings. Part of the house which he now occupies is the house in which Rachel (Searight) Stidger, the subject of this second memorial, entered, in the arms of her mother, in the spring of the year 1805, aged about six weeks. Hannah

43

was the wife of the late William B. Roberts, who left his home, at his country's call, to go to the Mexican war, and who died soon after the victorious army entered the City of Mexico. She and Mrs. Catherine Baker, her only living child, are now residents of South Bend, Indiana. Esther is the widow of C. B. Snyder, once a successful merchant in Fayette county, afterwards a prominent citizen and merchant in Philadelphia, Boston and New York. She, with two of her only living children, now reside in New York city.

Golden treasures to the living are pleasant memories of those who have lived life full well, and in ripened years of advanced age have passed from the weak bonds of frail mortality and the scenes of their earthly labors to life immortal, and to the world of eternal blessedness. Such was the life and departure from earth of Rachel (Searight) Stidger. She was quiet, gentle and patient, never neglecting a duty, nor failing in an act of kindness, or lacking on any occasion in any courtesy of life. Even as the sunbeam is composed of millions of smallest rays, so was her life made up of unnumbered thousands of acts of kindness, deeds of charity, kind looks, pleasant words and loving counsels. Her throne, her kingdom, her world was her home, where she ruled by affection and kindness.

Her life has spanned one of the most wonderful

periods in human history since the creation of the world. She was reared in the land where the ruins of fort and mound and temple of the dim mysterious Mound Builders were plain during her early and childhood years, and where likewise at the same time were to be seen the vestiges of villages and the traces of the war-path and camping grounds of the red lords of the forest, in a country they loved so well as a private hunting ground. These ruins, visible around the playground of her infancy, were the fading monuments of two of the most wonderful empires of the world—the Mound Builder and the Indian. The Mound Builders, a race with civilization but without history, stretched wide their realm from the Mississippi to the Alleghenies, and came either over Behring Strait, on its ice-bound floor, or fled from fabled Atlantis, when it was sinking in earthquake throes beneath the blue waves of the Atlantic. Without domestic animals they erected forts, great temples, altars, effigies, and tomb mounds. Southward and sunward they traveled after many generations of permanent residence, and were undoubtedly the architects and builders of the great halls, cities, temples, and the aqueducts of the Montezumas and the Incas of Peru. Their age corresponded with the stone and the beginning of the bronze period of Europe, and whether the ancient Mexicans and

Peruvians were their degenerated descendants, or that fever and famine, or plague swept them from off the face of the earth, we know not. We only know that in mystery was their origin, in power and civilization was their reign, and in darkness and gloom came their sad fate of decay and extinction.

The Indian who succeeded the Mound Builder was a race possessed of a tradition but having no civilization, and whose origin has been a fruitful subject of conflicting theories, which only agree in making him of Mongolian extraction, on account of the affinity of his language to that of the Tartar groups of languages. The Indian copied after the Mound Builder in flint and stone for rude weapons and crude utensils, while fort and mound only suggested to him stone pile graves, memorial heap, and stone circle, and the overgrown highways which he found were only partly reproduced in war-path and hunting trail.

Mrs. Searight's infancy and youth were passed when warrior and chief, like flitting shadows, were going to and fro on their way to see their great father at Washington. During her youthful days, she came in contact with that wonderful class of people of the Alleghenies, who were then pushing westward, where their courage and arms were destined to win the country from the Lakes to the Rio

Grande. Foremost as well as most numerous and always prominent in that western tide were the Scotch-Irish, the grandest self-asserting race that ever lived in the world. One of this noble race she married, in the person of William Searight, who, for honesty, sterling integrity, and an enduring name in the hearts of his fellow-citizens, has been scarcely paralleled, as was shown by the vast assemblage who came to his funeral to add their testimony to the lofty worth in life of the distinguished dead. Ere a score of years had passed over the head of the subject of this second memorial, she had witnessd the departure of the red lords of the forest, and the passing of the backwoodsmen to their mission of conquest in the valley of the Mississippi, and then was chosen as one of the young maidens who strewed flowers in the pathway of General Marquis de LaFayette when he passed through the county which bears his honored name. She was the last survivor of that little band of youth and beauty, and likewise amongst the last of the assembled hundreds at Uniontown who gazed upon General LaFayette, America's most honored guest and noblest friend. Frequently, in speaking of this interesting event, she has stated that she heard the smack of the kiss when General LaFayette and Albert Gallatin, then a distinguished resident of the county, met and greeted each other on the steps of the old court house of that day. After this, for a quarter of a century, she lived on the old National road, and witnessed in that time the full-orbed glory of stage coach travel wane and die before the iron pathway which, within her span of life, was to stretch throughout the land from ocean to ocean. During the next fifteen years, which only carried her from the prime of life to early old age, she witnessed the second stage of railroad growth and the rise and termination of the greatest civil war in the world's history. From the close of this war until the centennial year, she witnessed the resting period, as it were, of the nation, ere it moved forward in the van of modern progress of the world. From the centennial year until the close of her life, surrounded with kind friends and endearing relatives, she beheld an era unequaled in the world's advancement. During that time the phonograph had brought back the voices of those who had spoken, and had made their tones triumphant over time, death and the tomb; the telephone has annihilated distance in conversation, and electricity in a more pleasing form than as the storm fire of the heavens, has lighted up the gloom of night in city and town, while the imprisoned gases in the earth have been conducted into mansion and manufactory to afford heat and service without dust or ash.

Mrs. Rachel (Searight) Stidger, in her eighty-eight years of life, was signally fortunate in seeing more change of event, and of advancement in the material world and the history of the human race, than many of the untold millions of the past. Her life was consistent, pleasant and useful, and Time presented to her his most wonderful panorama of change and achievements. Reared amidst the ruins of two races, it was her privilege to witness the grandest triumphs of the third, the Anglo-Saxon, such as the birth of all the great American industries, and the development of one of the wonderful modes of modern travel, also not only the invention of, but also the adoption and growth of the telegraph, telephone and phonograph, and the development of electricity for light, heat and power. When her eyes first saw the light of day there was not an iron ploughshare in the whole world, nor was there a steamboat, steamship, locomotive nor railway train; telegraphing and telephoning were unknown; most of the inventions in machinery and nearly all the appliances for comfort and convenience were also unknown. The improvements in agriculture, mining, manufacturing, etc., were all made during the span of her life. What a privilege and yet what a responsibility to be permitted to live so long and witness so much. Like her sainted mother and her ancestors named, she was entombed

and over her grave was written the chilling word,
"died." Alongside this, however, thanks be to
God, were written the more cheering words, "to
be resurrected." In the fullness of years she has
passed to her reward, but has left us the precious
privilege of recalling and talking over the beautiful
story of her long life. Sweet as are the memories
of her long, useful and never to be forgotten life,
yet the scythe of time came to gather the ripened
sheaf into the garner. Around the scenes of her
infant childhood and girlhood days, death, in seem-
ing reluctance, came and whitened the ruddy cheek,
stilled the melodious tongue, dimmed the sparkling
eye, and hung a pale flag over the citadel of her
priceless heart. And yet how comforting it is to
feel and know that that same cold messenger in-
stantly and unhesitatingly held forth in his hand a
parchment signed by Him who knows that "we are
but dust," and "Who doeth all things well," and
whilst sadly reading the stern mandate, pointed to
a better life, "a house of many mansions," into
whose sacred portals he can never enter. How
beautiful and lovely it is to feel that in addition to
having been a friend to all the living, she was also
even a friend to the king of terrors himself. The
interment of her remains took place in Grace church
burying ground, Menallen township, on Saturday
afternoon, January 7th, 1893, from whose com-

50

BURIAL PLACE.

manding site can be seen, not very far distant to the eastward, the beautiful mountains over which, in her infancy, she came, and at the foot of which she lived her earliest and latest years, and also from where she was beckoned by the Redeemer, homeward, whither she frequently in angelic tones said she wanted to go.

Her funeral services were conducted by the Rector of St. Peter's Episcopal church, Uniontown, and the Rector of Christ's church, Brownsville. Notwithstanding the excessive coldness of the weather, large numbers of her old Uniontown friends and many others from the surrounding country assembled to witness the interment of her remains at Grace church, and were touched by the beautiful and solemn service, and by the rendering of the hymn "Nearer, My God, to Thee," which was sung by the choir during the interment. After her death, letters of condolence and tributes of respect to her Christian life and character were received by her children from many different parts of this and other States.

Those who would be like her must learn to follow in the footsteps of the Savior.

COL. T. B. SEARIGHT.

THEIR CHILDREN.

To William and Rachel (Brownfield) Searight (afterwards Stidger), the subjects of these memorials, were born six children, four sons and two daughters: Col. Thomas B., Ewing B., Mrs. Jean Shuman, Capt. William, James A., and Mrs. Elizabeth Colvin.

COL. THOMAS BROWNFIELD SEARIGHT.

The oldest in active practice of the lawyers at the Uniontown bar, is Col. Thomas Brownfield Searight, who was born on the National road, in Menallen township, Fayette county, Pennsylvania, February 20, 1827. He attended Washington and Jefferson college with James G. Blaine, and was graduated from that well-known institution of learning in the class of 1848, one year later than Blaine, who was one of his warm and intimate friends. He read law with James Veech, was admitted to the bar in 1850, and has been engaged in the practice of his profession ever since. He was editor of the *Genius of Liberty* from 1851 to 1861, and was elected as prothonotary in 1857, in 1860, in 1881

EWING B. SEARIGHT.

and in 1884, thus far being the only man in the county who has ever served four terms in that office. Colonel Searight was elected to the legislature in 1862 and again in 1864, served in the State senate from 1866 to 1868, and in 1873, without solicitation upon his part, was appointed by President Grant as surveyor-general of Colorado, which position he held for three years. He received the nomination for president judge in 1883, in the Fourteenth Judicial district of Pennsylvania, but dissension that year in the Democratic party prevented his election. Colonel Searight is a Jeffersonian Democrat. On October 29, 1857, he married Rose Flenniken, only daughter of Hon. Robert P. Flenniken, minister to Denmark under President Polk. Mr. Searight wrote a series of able and logical letters on "State Rights," and his forthcoming book, "The Old Pike," is pronounced by those competent to judge, a work of great value and of National interest.

EWING BROWNFIELD SEARIGHT.

One of the most popular and efficient superintendents of the National Road, or "Old Pike," is Ewing Brownfield Searight, who is the second son of William and Rachel (Brownfield) Searight, and was born at the village of Searights, in Menallen

JEAN (SEARIGHT) SHUMAN.

township, Fayette county, Pennsylvania, September 5, 1828. He received a good practical English education, and then engaged in agricultural pursuits, which he has followed successfully ever since. Mr. Searight is a man of standing in his community, and on February 3, 1859, married Elizabeth Jackson, only daughter of Zadoc Jackson. He is a democrat, an Episcopalian, has served as a township and county official, and was superintendent of the National Pike in Fayette county, by appointment of Governor Pattison, for two years, during which term he rendered the best of satisfaction.

JEAN (SEARIGHT) SHUMAN.

The third child and eldest daughter of William and Rachel (Brownfield) Searight, is Jean (Searight) Shuman, who was born in Menallen township, Fayette county, Pennsylvania, September 17, 1832. She received her education at Washington Female seminary, then under the charge of Mrs. Sarah R. (Foster) Hanna, who was a well-known teacher and a prominent member of the Seceder church, of western Pennsylvania. On April 25, 1849, she married Capt. Thomas Shuman, of Brownsville, who died February 11, 1878. Some fifteen years after her husband's death Mrs. Shuman removed to Uniontown, where she has resided ever since.

CAPT. WILLIAM SEARIGHT.

One of the best local newspaper editors that
Pennsylvania ever produced was Capt. William
Searight, who had served bravely in the late civil
war, and was popular wherever he was known, on
account of genial nature and generous impulses.
He was the third son of William and Rachel
(Brownfield) Searight, and was born at Searights,
in Menallen township, Fayette county, Pennsylvania, July 28, 1835. He received his education
in Dunlap's Creek academy, and Washington and
Madison colleges, and after serving for some time
as a clerk, in 1853 was appointed as a cadet to
West Point Military academy, from which he re-
signed one year later. He then took a thorough
commercial course, was in clerical employ under
Governor Black, of Nebraska, and then became a
clerk under his brother in the prothonotary's office
at Uniontown. The late civil war came, and he
left his clerkship and comfortable home, to enlist
in Co. G, 8th Pennsylvania reserves, Captain Oliphant. He was made first sergeant, soon became
popular, and his West Point knowledge made him
an efficient drill officer. Upon Captain Oliphant's
promotion, he was elected captain over several of
the company officers who were his seniors in rank.
Sickness compelled him to resign, but after return-

ELIZABETH SEARIGHT ' COLVIN.

ing home and recruiting his health, he enlisted again, as a private soldier, in the 88th Pennsylvania regiment, and served until the close of the war. Under President Johnson's administration he served efficiently as a departmental clerk at Washington city, and in 1869 became local editor of the *Genius of Liberty*. In his new sphere of labor he became phenominally successful, and made the *Genius* one of the ablest and most popular local newspapers of the State. From that time on, until his death in 1881, Capt. William (familiarly known as " B ") Searight did splendid local work on the *Genius, Standard* and *Democrat* at Uniontown, and was a valued correspondent of several Pittsburg dailies. He passed away July 31, 1881 : his remains were interred at Grace church, under the auspices of the Grand Army of the Republic, but his memory will long survive in many loving hearts, on account of his many generous and noble qualities.

ELIZABETH (SEARIGHT) COLVIN.

The youngest child of William and Rachel (Brownfield) Searight is Elizabeth (Searight) Colvin, who was born at Searights, in Menallen township, Fayette county, Pennsylvania, February 17, 1839. She received her education at Washington Female seminary, then under charge of Mrs. Sarah

JAMES A. SEARIGHT.

R. (Foster) Hanna, a Scotch-Irish teacher of ability
and reputation. On February 7, 1859, she married
Joseph T. Colvin, who is now President of the
Pittsburg National Bank of Commerce. Mr. and
Mrs. Colvin have resided ever since their marriage
in Pittsburg.

JAMES ALLISON SEARIGHT.

James Allison Searight, President of the Peoples Bank of Fayette County, and the first member of the Scotch-Irish Congress of America,
from Southwestern Pennsylvania, is the youngest son of William and Rachel (Brownfield) Searight, and was born on the old Searight homestead, in Menallen township, Fayette county, Pennsylvania, September 13, 1836. He received his
academic education at Dunlap's Creek Presbyterian
academy, and after spending some time at the Iron
City Business college of Pittsburg, he entered
Kenyon college, Gambier, Ohio, where he was a
classmate of E. L. Stanton, son of the great war
secretary, Edwin M. Stanton. Mr. Searight was
graduated from Kenyon college in 1863, and two
years later entered the Philadelphia Divinity
school, which ill health compelled him to leave in
a short time. He passed two years in Washington
city, and in 1871 established himself at Uniontown, this State, in his present insurance and real

estate office. Mr. Searight is a member of St. Peter's Protestant Episcopal church, has been very active in the affairs of the church, and has served repeatedly in diocesan councils and conventions. He helped, in 1873, to organize the Peoples Bank of Fayette County, of which he was elected the first cashier, and of which he has served as President since 1889. Mr. Searight has spent considerable time and been at some expense in securing data for an accurate account in which to preserve for all time to come the memory of his family and ancestry.

www.ingramcontent.com/pod-product-compliance
Lightning Source LLC
Chambersburg PA
CBHW022017080426

42733CB00007B/638